In the Midst of the Storm and Life Struggles

My Life in Poems

In the Midst of the Storm and Life Struggles

My Life in Poems

By

Alicia Denise Hall Jackson

All In All Publishing
2146 E. River Trace Dr. #7
Memphis, TN 38134
www.allinallpublishing.com

ISBN #978-1-7323749-8-0

Printed in the United States of America

First Printing, 2019

Dedication

I would like to dedicate this book to the ones that supported, believed, and helped me along the way to make this possible. Your love and encouragement really pushed me to write and finish this book. Thank you:

To my children, Shakia, Amir, and Tevion

My husband, Joseph

My mother, Gloria Jean Wilson

All of the domestic violence victims and single mothers all over the world

Acknowledgments

I would like to acknowledge God first and foremost for giving me the ability, strength, knowledge, and experience to write this book. I would like to acknowledge and thank my spiritual leaders: The late Elder Thomas Jennings Sr., Bishop Leslie Williams Sr., Elder Johnnie L. Bradley Sr., Elder Tommie Scruggs Sr., the late Mother Verna Simms, the late Mother Dorothy Sullivan and First Lady Vergie Scruggs. I would like to acknowledge Mrs. Yvomming Humphrey, Ms. Dana Williams, Ms. Jerline Williams, Ms. Keona Washington, my best friend: the late Latesia Dye McIntyre (Tish), my friend the late Chandra Wells-Williams(Shun Mo), My father, Mr. Lee Hodges Jr., My father, Mr. Lacye V. Knowles(Bebe), Mr. Randall Smith, and my mother in law: the late, Francis Jackson Hall. I would also like to acknowledge the following people: my aunts Callie Cox, Kathleen Cox, Jeraldine Calvin, Shirley Curtis and Lena Taylor; My grandmother: the late Louise Cox; my sisters: Lakevia Hall and Tadasha Scott; my godsister: Carol Walls; Lady Daphne Freeman Bradley; my cousins Tanika Taylor Smith and Koresa Taylor; all of my uncles, aunts, grandparents, nephews, cousins and nieces; Jerald Brown with All In All Publishing; Mrs. Annie Dickerson; a special acknowledgement to a young lady that I met by the name of Nikki Shun that sowed a special seed towards helping me to get my book published; a special acknowledgement to Marcus D. Porter for doing my photo shoot, Tinelle White for doing my makeup, and Jonae for doing my hair; and last but not least the late Maya Angelou who inspired me to write poetry. Thanks everyone that had a positive impact in my life.

Forward

My name is Alicia Denise Hall Jackson. I was born on January 5, 1975 in Memphis, Tn. under the parentage of AK Hall Jr. and Gloria Jean Cox Hall Wilson. My mother raised me as a single parent. Even though she was married to my father when I was born, he wasn't present in my life to help raise me. I met my father when I was around 11 or 12 years old and I was very excited! He bought me ice cream, took my mother and I to the fair, and also to Piccadilly restaurant. Those are the only memories that I have of him. After that visit, I haven't seen or heard from him again. Not having my father in my life really took a toll on me. I went through a lot of emotional and mental stress. But my mother has been there for me since day one.

I thank God for allowing her to be in my life and never leaving me. I know it wasn't easy being a single mother; she's always been a great inspiration to me because through all that she's been through, she never gave up on herself or me. Not having my father in my life made me feel very unwanted by him. I used to think, *What did I do to deserve this type of treatment?* Later in life I was told that he was physically, mentally and emotionally abusive to my mother. Through her own personal changes, my mother did the best that she could to care for my sister and I. We never went without shoes on our feet, clothes on our backs, and food on the table. That's because God made a way for our mother to provide for us.

Through my adolescent and teenage years I turned to older men for the lack of attention I had missed out on from not having my father around; it seemed to fill a void. When my mother would drop me off at school, I would cut class to spend time with those older male figures. I started having sex at an early age and I developed a bad habit of running away from home just to be with whoever I was dealing with. My first sexual experience was in jr. high school and I caught a very bad disease called Trichomoniasis. I didn't know what was happening at that time but I was feeling bad and being very irritable. I told my mother about how I was feeling and once she took me to the doctor, that's when we knew what it was. I felt so bad for taking myself, my mother and my family through that. But nevertheless, running away from home became a sort of ritual: one time I ran away and got hit by a car while trying to avoid getting a whooping. I suffered from a concussion, a busted eye and busted mouth. I don't remember anything about the accident but I was told I went through the windshield. Another time I ran away I ended up getting severely raped while I was on my cycle. My mother ended up taking me to the hospital and the doctors told me that I would never be able to get pregnant or have children. My pattern of running away lead me to juvenile court and eventually locked up. Then my mother felt the need to admit me into a mental facility. I felt like that was the worst thing a mother could do to her child. But being away from my family helped me to see the things that I was doing wrong.

During my stay in the mental hospital, God started using me to express myself through writing and poetry. I used to always keep a journal to write down how I felt. I didn't realize that God was dealing with me, but I had a praying mother, grandmother and family in my life and those prayers were being answered. When you've been raised in a holy church (although I hated going as a teenager because I felt it was a waste of time), you can't help but to pray and ask God to help you through tough times and situations. With my sister looking up to me and a family that relied on me, I needed to make some real changes. The battle with flesh and selfish, lustful desires became a war in itself.

I graduated from high school in 1993 and at 18 I thought I was grown, as most teenagers think. A few months after graduation, I got accepted to Atlanta Job Corps for the CNA program. I was so excited because I had always wanted to become a nurse (my two main passions were to become a nurse and to be a poet). Job Corps would be a good experience of being away from home and starting a new life for myself. But I also felt the loneliness at times from being away from my family. While in Job Corps I was dealing with the death of my grandmother, Louise Cox. She greatly inspired me, and she was the backbone of my life and our family; one of the sweetest ladies you could have ever met or have been around. I met a lot of different people while in the program, which was easy for me because I've always been a people person. I learned how to be more independent in everyday life while I was there. We were able to receive passes to leave the center on certain days and times. When I was comfortable being in Atlanta, I started back meeting older men. I met one in particular and we developed a relationship and ended up getting married. I became pregnant with our first child, a daughter who I named Shakia. He started out treating me how a young lady should be treated: buying nice things, taking me out, telling me all of the things that made me love him more. But after a while, the abuse started; physically, mentally and emotionally. I didn't know what I could have done for him to start treating me so bad, but I stayed with him in hopes things would change.

I endured several miscarriages before receiving my second bundle of joy named Amir on February 10, 2002. I was separated from my then husband at the time I delivered my son. But God and my family was still there for me during that period. A few days after I had him, we had to rush Amir to the emergency room. He had very short breathing going on and was really sick. He developed some health issues that still affect him to this day. After Amir, I became pregnant a year later with my third child, Tavion. My husband and I weren't on good terms, but we were all under the same roof. He was still being abusive. Then I started noticing things were missing in our home. Not only appliances and jewelry, but even our son's pampers! This is when I found out that my husband was on drugs badly. I even found a crack pipe in our bathroom but I didn't know that's what it was at the time because I had never been exposed to one. I felt so hurt and alone and I stayed in a depressed state over time. But yet, I stayed with him.

We tried to have a stable life in Georgia for our family but it would only last for so long. At times things were good, at others things were worse. We would separate over and over again every two years. My children and I went through a lot. We moved around quite a bit and during those moves, we lost several of our material things. We finally moved back to Memphis in 2011. I missed being in Georgia because I met a lot of great people there over the years and I had a wonderful church family. I love them so much for supporting my children and I over those difficult times. My husband had talked me into letting him back into our lives once again after a couple of years being separated and again, thinking I wanted to keep our family together, I let him back in. I had high hopes that we would work out this time, but eventually, the abuse reappeared. So I separated from him again and this time, I became homeless. This was a difficult time for my children and I. The depression came on stronger than ever before. We were living from place to place, hotel to hotel for about 6 months. Then with the help of God, I found a way to file and gain my divorce. When it was over, I finally felt free! It had been like I was drowning but I was rescued from it. And even after the divorce, my ex-husband still attempted to control and abuse me!

I met, fell in love with and remarried the love of my life on Christmas day, 2016. His name is Joseph Laroyce Jackson, Sr. That was one of the happiest days of my life! He had gone through similar situations of physical, mental and emotional abuse as well. He gave his life to God on the day of our wedding. I thank God for my husband! He's been a blessing to me and my children. I never thought anyone could love me and my children after all of the hardships we've had to encounter. We have our moments of issues between us, but we remember to put God first and foremost so we can conquer through it all! That's what has brought me this far. I wrote this book to inspire everyone who I come across. Whatever battles and hardships you have in your lives, you can make it with the help of God. So please, please, please don't ever give up! I even battle with giving up at various times but God is always there to remind me that He will see me through! There has never been a time that God has failed me. So hold onto God's unchanging hand. Always stay faithful to God and always pray. Prayer changes things no matter how dark it looks in life. I hope this book inspires someone. If He did it for me, He can and will do it for you! Remember that God is a habit breaker, no matter if it's drugs, lust, lying, stealing, cheating, adultery, fornication and any type of abuse. As my First Lady always says, "Keep looking up!!!" Thank you and God bless!

Table of Contents

In Prison 20 Years but Not Sentenced

In the hands

Of a person who's supposed to be a man

That controlled, abused and deceived me for 20 whole years

Yes, it brought me so, so many tears

Tears of hurt and pain

And strength that I was hoping to gain

Gaining strength from walking away from the abuse

But I just said to myself, "Oh, what's the use?"

What's the use in leaving

Because I had lost all hope and self-esteem as a woman

I was feeling like there wasn't anybody else out there for me

Blinded, I couldn't see

I couldn't see through all of the physical, mental and emotional abuse

Because I had put so much trust and hope in you

But much violently, you grew

You grew with so much abuse, anger and rage

Yes, you really did set the stage

The stage of not caring and loving me anymore

Yes indeed, you put on a great big show

A show of betraying who you really are

And of you taking off that mask of deceit and lies

And you giving me no replies

No replies to why you treated me this way

And me not wanting to stay

Not staying in this prison of abuse anymore

And I know God must truly have something great in store

Because He's allowing me to see that I'm someone that truly adores

Adoring me for who I am to Him

And Him opening up my blinded eyes I used to have

Yes, I'm finally free

From your prison of abuse after so many years

I'm just thanking God and shedding so many tears

The tears of peace, love, hope and joy

Now I can see what God really has in store

In store for me in letting me live

Through all the hurt, sorrow, abuse and pain

And Him taking away all of the shame

The shame of staying in this mess so very long

Now I'm heading towards another zone

A zone of hope, joy and peace

And me living life so much at ease

Ease from those prison walls of abuse and hopelessness

And me never looking back to selfishness

Selfishness of not wanting better for myself

Because I deserve it and so much more

God indeed is a man that I will always truly, truly adore
Adoring God for bringing me out
And not giving up on me
And blinded, I used to be

The Calling of the Night

The calling of the night
As you hear the beating of my heart
All during the dark
The burning of my chest
Brought me less rest
The slamming of the door
Which I say to myself
I should hear no more
The sweating of my hands
Brought me such great demands
I need the feeling of being comforted
And not the feeling of being alone
The dreams I have at night
Brings me much fright
The dreams I have at night
Brings me much fright
The dreams that come to me
Makes me feel so insecure
Then again, it makes me more mature
The calling of the night is my biggest fright

Say No!!!!

Say no to drugs
Or you'll become a thug
Say no to violence
Or you'll get less allowance
Say no to all evil
And you'll become a great believer
A believer in Jesus Christ
And you should get Him in your life
A life of hope and salvation
And it shouldn't be no hesitation

One day In Time

One day in time as each day goes by
One day in time as I begin to cry
One day in time as I begin to wonder why
One day in time as the stars begin to shine
One day in time my life is all mines
One day in time I'll have many dreams
One day in time I'll begin to do many, many things
One day in time the bells begin to ring, ring, and ring!!!

Being Loved

Being loved is like a dove
It's from the Almighty God from up above
Being loved eases the pain
Which really doesn't remain
Being loved makes you feel good
Just like you should
Being loved is something worth giving
And being loved makes you feel like you're something worth living

For The Love of You

For the love of you, it's very true
For the love of you, I really knew
That it was meant for us to be together
For always and forever
For the love of you
We shall live in peace
And be at ease
For the love of you
Our love is growing stronger by the day
In each and every way
So please let's continue to pray

Your Love

Your love is like a river that flows with waters of joy
Your kindness is as sweet as a dove
And it's from the Almighty God above
Your friendship is a special thing
That you could ever give to another human being
Your smile is as beautiful as a flower
And you keep giving it every hour

Gentle Blessings

As gentle blessings follow pain
It's this joy I hope to regain
The gentle blessings I know
That beat in the winter wheat
Then the same things repeat

Thank You, Lord

Thank You, Lord for my life

Thank You, Lord for my wife

Thank You, Lord for the birds that sing

Just thank you Lord for everything!!!

Everything that You have made on this beautiful Earth

Even the waters in the ocean that we surf

Surfing the deep blue waters in the ocean

Just thanking You, Lord, for just that small portion

Because everything that You do, Lord, is more than a notion

A notion of the past, present, and future

And You keep on making a way because You are the final solution

Going On

Going on
As the map has shown
Going on
To which zone
Going on
To the east or to the west
Going on
Puts you through a test
Going on
To your many destinations
Going on
Is a great sensation
Going on
Is a feeling of relief
Going on
Is one of my beliefs
P.S.: North, South, East, West

Never Give Up

Never give up as time goes by

Never give up when crime is nearby

Never give up when you have such big disappointments

But just remember, it's just for a moment

Never give up when things seem so bad

Just remember that God is on your side

And He doesn't hide

Never give up when people put you down

Because they're not the one who's going to be wearing the crown

Never give up when you're depressed

So remember that God can make it much less!!!!

When You're Down

When you're down
Just take off the sad little frown
And God will make you happy as a clown
Though sometimes it seems like there's no hope at all
Just remember that you can't continue to fall

The Tears of Pain

Sometimes I just sit down and cry
And wonder if life is passing me by
There is so much I don't understand
And I wish I had a helping hand
I need to be shown the things that I'm longing for
And I wish that things was like they were before

No Way Out

I'm trapped in a room all alone
With no one to call on
My heart is filled with much despair
And I really need someone to care
The tears that I cry out brings me much pain
And it seems to remain
I don't know what to do
I'm so lost, lonely, and blue

My Sadness

My sadness is a symbol of pain
It seems to me it remains the same
It just seems like it's not real
It's only a game
Then I talk to the Lord
Then I begin to cry
Then I begin to wonder why
I've just cried until I couldn't cry anymore
But I just try to ignore
It's hard trying to ignore something that's there
Then I begin to say my daily prayer

The Lost

I've lost all hope, joy, and peace
And I'm not really at ease
My heart is broken into a million pieces
The love that I used to have is all gone
And it is such a heavy tone
My heart beats faster and faster
Day by day
I do think that I need to pray
I cry out the tears of pain
And everything seems to remain

Halloween

Halloween, Halloween
What does it really mean?
Does it mean
Making pumpkin pies?
And telling no lies?
Does it mean dressing up in many costumes?
Or just listening to many scary tunes?
Tell me
What does Halloween really mean?

PUSH

Pray Until Something Happens

Pray-when you can't see your way out

God can and will make a way out of no way

Until-until you give it up to God

And letting Him be in charge

So that He's able to do his job

Something-something has to happen

Remember that God may not come when you want Him to

But remember He's always on time

Happens-meaning whatever happens, God has the last and final say

And just remember, He's going to make a way

P.S.: just remember to PUSH!!!

The Struggle

Going through the struggle is such a big test
But remember that God can and will make it much less
Going through the struggle sometimes
Brings on great challenges
But God can give you
His strength during that great big hour
Going through the struggle sometimes causes pain
But remember that God will give you strength to sustain
And nothing really remains the same

Being a Woman

Being a woman is such a beautiful thing to be
For she's a strong individual
She's meek and humble
And she never goes down without a fight
For she tries constantly with all her might
She's a great go getter
And she's hardly ever bitter
She's open minded and always keeping the faith
And she's always praying, keeping the devil away
Being a Woman!!!!

God's Gift of Life

God's gift of life has been given to us
And in Him we can find trust
Trusting Him in everything that we do and say
Oh yes! He can and will make a way
Making a way out of no way when it seems
That everything has been turned inside out
Without a doubt
He is working it out
Working out the problem and situation
Without having any hesitation
Having any hesitation to do what He promised He will do
And making all of your dreams really come true

Getting Back to That Place

Getting back to that place in finding myself

Getting back to that place in not worrying to death

Getting back to that place in not being broken

Because as you know that the word has already been spoken

And it is the greatest token

The greatest token that you'll ever find

And it will continue to be on your mind

A New Beginning

A new beginning in living and loving life

A new beginning in letting go of all of the strife

A new beginning in letting go of all the hurt, sorrow, and pain

A new beginning is what I hope to gain

I hope to gain more joy, love and peace

And to be very at ease

Being at ease in my mind

And continuing to let my light shine

Just Because

Just because I'm in need
Doesn't mean that you're in the lead
The lead of having all of the success
And living daily in much distress
Distress of how I'm going to survive
And praying to God to keep me alive!!!!!

You’ve Taken

You’ve taken so much from me

And yes, blinded I used to be

I used to be blinded by your mental and physical

Abuse and mistreatment

But now you’re going to be the one that’s going to be reaping

Reaping all of the hurt, sorrow and pain

That you’ve brought to my life

And I won’t have any more strife

Not having any more strife in my heart

Yes, you’re the one who tore us apart

Apart from a great family and a happy home

You chose to go to another zone

A zone of deceit and destruction

And living your life of torment and corruption

If Only You Knew

If only you knew the pain that I feel inside
No longer can I really hide
Hide the torment and pain that I'm feeling in my heart
Right now I just feel so torn apart
Apart from life itself of not having all my needs being met
Sometimes I just feel like saying, "Oh what the heck!"
What the heck in keeping the faith
I know that I really do need to pray
Pray that God gets me out of this rut
Before I begin to self-destruct

Your Breakthrough

Your breakthrough is knocking at the door
But you say to yourself
I just can't take anymore
You fast and pray
But it still doesn't seem that God is making a way
You begin to talk to the Lord
Over and over about your situation
And you say, "Lord, please don't make a hesitation"
No hesitation in solving the problem
You're doing what needs to be done
And going so far and beyond

FAMILY

Family plays a special part in your everyday life
Especially the ones without all of the strife
Having someone to uplift and not tear you down
Someone who will lift you when you're falling to the ground
Someone that's very true
True in everything that they say and do
Someone who will help you figure out that next big clue
A clue of togetherness and wholeness
A clue of having a lot of boldness
Boldness to tell you when you're wrong
Boldness so that one day you will be able
To set upon that throne
That throne of glory
As we know, we all have a story
A story of heartaches and pain
But through Jesus Christ, His strength we will gain

My Three Angels

My three angels, oh how I love you all
Because you're the ones who make me stand up so very tall
Standing tall in myself and not giving up
You're the one who gives me so much support
Supporting me in my everyday life
And not making me have any more strife
Strife against the ones that do me wrong
But yet and still, you're the ones who set the tone
The tone of my life in keeping me grounded
And always in prayer
Oh yes! I do declare
I declare each and every one of you
For making me who I am
Making me the woman after God's own heart
And keeping this family from not falling apart
My three angels (Shakia, Amir, Tevion)

I'm Sorry

I'm sorry for all the pain I've seen you go through

But Boo, if only you knew

Knew that I tried to do my best in keeping the family together

But I guess it just didn't get any better

In better in our finances, our emotions and pain

But things just can't remain the same

FALL

Such a beautiful time of the year

Especially when the air is so much clearer

Looking at the beautiful and colorful leaves fall down from the tree

And just feeling so very free

Free as nature takes it's course

With me beginning to get so very hoarse

Hoarse from me playing and shouting in so many leaves

So then I began to get up and roll up my sleeves

Rolling up my sleeves from having so much fun

And living life as the bright shining sun

Will I

Will I ever get my life back again?
Becoming that bright, vibrant woman who I used to be?
So full of life, hope, and dreams
Dreaming of having so many things
Having and making all of my means met
Not having any regret
Not regretting saying, “I would have” or “I should have”
Done this or that
Living and loving life to the fullest
Leaving everyone else clueless
Clueless of how I got this and how I got that

When I Need You The Most

You are always there to show me that you care
You care about all my needs and my well being
You care for me even when I was blind and couldn't see
I couldn't see how the way was going to be made
But yet and still I prayed
Praying that you will give me strength to sustain
And your joy I hope to gain
And my dignity to remain
Remain the same
As you take away all the hurt, sorrow and pain
Because my joy I must proclaim

The GMC Channel (Gospel 189)

The GMC Channel
Is truly an inspirational channel
That I look at each and everyday
Praying to God to make a way
Make a way to uplift my heart and soul
And pray that I stay in control
Stay in control of my daily life struggles
And listening to all the great music artists
As they bring beautiful melodies to my heart
And me not falling apart
Apart in facing what's to come in the day
And continuing to pray

It's Near

The blessings are nearer than I think
And I just can't sink
Sink from all of the sleepless nights
And not going down without a fight
All of the fighting that I have to encounter
And keeping my light shining like a glowing lantern
A lantern that lights the room with so much joy, hope, and peace
And not being worried in the least
Not worried about how it's going to come
And just staying real calm
Calm in my spirit and in my heart
Trying not to fall apart

Don't Quit, Keep Fighting

She keeps fighting with all her might
And she's not giving up without a fight
She's fighting to stay as she continues to survive
Survive through all the good times
As well as the bad
But sometimes she does get a little sad
Sad from so much hurt, struggle, and pain
And her joy she hopes will remain
Striving to keep her head up
And praying to God to get her out of that rut
A rut of frustration and confusion
Because sometimes to her it's an illusion
An illusion to what's to come in her near future
And her heart is getting stitched with a great big suture
From all the pain and torment
Now she's going on with her life to finally represent
Representing where God has brought her from
And living her life so far and beyond
Beyond her hopes and dreams
Finally getting back her high self-esteem
An esteem that was once taken

Now she's a great star in the making

Can't Wait

I can't wait until the day comes for us to be happy again
Without worrying for a place of our own
A place we can finally call home
Without worrying or looking for any good thing
We're finally waking up out of this terrible dream
A dream of heartaches and pain
Gaining strength in our hearts, minds, bodies and souls
And the enemy not having any more control

These Four Walls

Sometimes I feel so trapped and all alone
Not having anyone to call on
I pray, I cry, I talk to God
But nothing seems to happen at that time
I really do need to unwind
Unwind
From having so much on my mind
And in my heart
And yes, I do need a new start
From these four walls
Because I just can't continue to fall

She's Crying Out

She's crying out
From all the hurt, sorrow and pain
That's in her heart
And she's praying to be set apart
Apart from all the mental and emotional abuse
And not having an excuse
An excuse of not wanting to go on with her life
To be able to let go of all the strife
Strife from the ones who put her down
And strife from the ones who sometimes make her frown
Frown from so much pain
But strength she hopes to truly gain

It Still Hurts

It still hurts that you're not here
But each and every day it gets much clearer
Clearer in my heart, mind, body and soul
Because yes, I need to be consoled
Consoled with your warm embrace of love and tender care
Caring about me as a daughter from her father
And loving me even harder
Harder as the days go by
I sometimes begin to cry
Cry from a broken heart because you're not here with me
I keep wondering what tore us apart
I wish we were off to a brand new start
A start of restoration and hope
And that you would never elope
P.S.: I miss you, daddy!!!!

I See You In Me

Growing up is what we had to do
Because we really didn't have a clue
A clue of us being raised up only by our loving mothers
And finding faults in others
Finding faults in so many others
Because our birth fathers weren't there
To show us that they really do care
Caring about our needs and wants
Teaching us the do's and don'ts
Teaching us to be great daughters and sons
Playing and having lots of fun
Having lots of fun going to major basketball games
I guess they really were ashamed
Ashamed of showing us off to the people they loved most
To us, I guess we were like ghosts
Ghosts of the heartaches and pain
We were wishing our fathers would've remained
In our lives
But instead they've set up so much strife
Because they've never really been part of our lives
Getting to know us as sweet daughters and sons

Instead they left us with our moms
Who had to pick up the broken pieces in our lives
And praying that God removes all the hurt and strife
Remove all the hurt and strife from our heart
Continuing to set us apart

Written for myself and my nephew (Omari Hall)

Regardless

Regardless of how you to may have came
The love I have for you will always remain
Remain in my heart and never let it depart
Because it's the beginning of a very new start
A new start of motherhood all over again
Raising you two as I intend
Into a very nice, warm and loving home
Oh yes, you two will really set the tone
In making me stand so very strong
Because of the way you both came into the world
You two are mommy and daddy's sweet little girls
Loving like your mom
Hardcore like your dad
What a combination you two truly are
You both make us so glad
Glad to get to know your ways and thoughts
Thankful that you don't blame us for all of our faults
Faults of sin and lust
We pray to God that we will indeed have trust
Trusting Him to forgive us for all our sins
And yes, living life as God intends

Mommy and daddy love you both

RJ1 and RJ2

FINALLY

Finally, a place to call home
Because we've been in so many time zones
Going and living from place to place
Lord, we just couldn't continue to run that big race
Of living there in Georgia
Then back to Memphis
Every other year or two
We were all beginning to get and feel so very blue
In our hearts and minds
Please Lord, we prayed to let Your light shine
Let Your light shine on us
Because in You we found so much trust
Trusting You in what You promised You were going to do
Oh yes, you lead us to that big clue
Of living in our own place
It has so much space!
Compared to living in that one room all together
But we stood through all of that stormy weather
Finally a place to call home

I Never Would Have Thought

I never would have thought
That I would have been in a marriage like this
I wanted marital bliss
Bliss from all the hurt, sorrow, pain and lust
But there's no more trust
From neither one of us
All of the dreams we had turned to dust
Dust of deceit and lies
With neither one of us sharing our replies
Of what went wrong
Now we're on different zones
Zones of going our separate ways
Although we've had so many delays
Of our needs and some of our wants
With us telling our kids the do's and don'ts
Of being in a faithful marriage and relationship
So we need to get a grip
On what we're going to do
Because trust me
I won't continue to be blue
In this marriage with you

I have to figure out my next clue
Of going on with my life
And letting go of the hurt, sorrow and strife
In my heart
Yes, I believe we need to be apart
I really do need a brand new start
In my life
To become someone else's wife
Who deserves my love and heart
And who won't tear us apart

TIRED

I'm tired of all of the mental and emotional abuse
That I encounter each and every day
I pray to God that He'll make a way
Of escape from all of the hurt, sorrow, and pain
His strength I'm hoping to truly regain
While gaining more self-motivation and hope in my mind
Please!!! I just need to unwind
From all of the abusive relationships
Looking far beyond that big eclipse
Of being in a happy relationship
And marriage again some day
But I will continue to pray
To never, ever go astray
From the love of God
And never letting anyone tear us apart

You Don't Know My Story

Because I'm giving God all the glory
That's due to Him for bringing me out
Of so many situations and circumstances
And for giving me so many chances
Chances to live and not to die
Sometimes I still cry
From having a broken heart
Because of so many people who tore us apart
From having that trust and love
Oh yes, it does come from God from up above
Above the heavens and under the earth
I need to be rebirthed
From all the hurt, sorrow, and pain
For God's strength I will gain
In Him I pray to stay sustained
In my heart and my mind
I'll keep praying a thousand more times
I will pray
Because I know He's making a way
He's making a way and sometimes I can't see
It will be a way out of no way

So I just can't go astray
From God's love and faith
Because in Him it is safe

No Strings Attached

I'm doing it on my own
With the help of God
Leaning and depending on Him with my all
Praying each and every day
And keeping the faith
Standing up so strong and tall
While not continuing to fall
In not asking for your help and support anymore
The Lord is the One I truly, truly adore
Adoring His love and tender mercies
That He shows me each and every day
Oh yes, He's making a way
Out of no way
No, I couldn't see
But one day soon
I will be
That bright, independent young lady
That the Lord is calling for
With Him blessing me ever the more
In my heart, mind, body and soul
I won't let the devil take control

Of what belongs to me
My blinded eyes are open
Now I can see
God's great work at hand
I'm praying for his strength to stand
Bold and firm
On His promises
Of what He has for me
Yes, I decree
The blessings of the Lord
And all His riches and glory
Because He left me here to tell the story
Of what He's done for me
And of living my life so free
From all of life's stresses
He's given me so many blessings
On every hand
So I must continue to stand
On the Word of God
Praying to never, ever, ever depart

Blue Lights Flashing

I looked to my left and they were there
On every corner as I drove down the street
I'm really feeling much defeat
I'm getting pulled over because I have no tags
Because I lack the means to do what needs to be done
So yes, I was on the run
From getting caught by the police
I need some peace
So I can be settled and at ease
In my heart, mind, body and soul
I can't let this situation take control
Of my emotions
I need to pray and say my daily devotions
To keep me grounded
And protected
From hurt, harm and danger
So I won't continue to run into strangers

Never Looking Back

Never looking back to that place
Of brokenness, hurt, confusion and deceit
Because things just can't continue to repeat
Repeating all the torment, pain
And lack of realness in my life
Mostly from all of the people who set up so much strife
From all the lies that was told
And unfaithfulness that was shown
By their actions and ways
I feel so betrayed
In my soul, mind and heart
Yes, unfaithfulness tore us apart
From having the stable relationship we once had
Sometimes I still feel a little sad
From all the lies
And from your end, no replies
To the hurt you've caused in my life
I finally let go of all the strife
That was once lingering in my heart
Now I'm off to a brand new start
Starting my life all over again

From beginning to the end
I will never look back
To that place where I once been

No More Lies

Promises after promises
Are what you say
Getting these kids' hopes up so high
While continually telling them those black, awful lies
Being lowdown, hateful, and deceitful
But they will not be in defeat
Nor mistreated
From the being of you
No, you don't even have a clue
Of the envy that's in their hearts
But you're the one that tore this family apart
For not standing up and being the man
Sometimes I feel like climbing and running up a tree
The tree of comfort and support
Now we have to move out of this rut
Moving to a place such as New York
A city of happiness, hopes, and dreams
With us living life at higher extremes
Of what's to come
And not having to run
Running from the fear of getting hurt again

While you continue to live your life in sin

Breaking Through The Walls

Breaking through the walls of defeat
Just relaxing in God and giving Him all the heat
Of life's stress
While pushing through these big tests
Of not giving up hopes and dreams
And believing and trusting God for my all
Through all the hurt, pain and disappointments
I realize that it's only for a moment
In time
I will let my light shine
Shining so bright I will continue to fight
Fight in getting what belongs to me
Yes indeed, I do decree
All of my heart's desire
And telling the devil that he is a lie
A lie of all his tricks and trades
I won't be joining in his parade
Of self-destruction and depression
I'm living life as a viewer's discretion
Of what's to come
And living life to the bright, early morn

HELPLESS???

Helpless is how I'm feeling right now
I don't have the proper means
To care for myself and my children
I want to take care of their needs and wants
I want them to have the finer things in life
Such as a nice, peaceful home
And for them to live in their own comfort zone
Of love and peace, joy and happiness
Around the home
Because of being unstable and unsettled
For almost a year
And yes, they've shed tears
From watching our home fall apart
While praying for a peaceful and happy start
Having a God fearing good life
Of hope and happiness and not being depressed
And having less stress
And being able to rest

Been There, Done That

I've been there and done that
Living from place to place
And not having anywhere to go
Praying to God to give me clarity
And directions in what to do
Because at this point I don't even have a clue
Of what's to come
Because I live so far and beyond
My wildest dreams and imaginations
But I'm holding my head up
Without having any hesitations
Of what to do with my life
But I'm praying to God to completely take away
All of the hurt and all of the strife

Women of Faith

Women of faith
Continue to run God's race
With much grace
Grace in having more wisdom and knowledge
In wearing many hats
Of faith, hope, and strength
And continuing to turn to God to vent
And having Him represent
His best
Giving you His strength
To continue to endure those great big tests

Dear Lord, Save Our Youth

Dear Lord, save our youth
Because they're falling by the waist side
Each and every day
I know, Lord, that You will make a way
Please Lord, open their eyes and let them see
That they can be all that they really want to be
Let them strive to be their best
And Lord, let them pass those great big tests
Of peer pressure in wanting to fit into the crowd
And let them find their voice to shout it out loud
Don't let them be afraid to be different from the rest
And let them stand bold through all great tests

Taking Back What The Devil Stole From Us

Taking back what the devil stole from us
In God we trust
With our all
Staying prayed up to continue not to fall
In hopelessness and fearfulness
So continue to trust God because it is a twist
In putting on more love, joy, peace and strength
We must keep a pure heart to repent
Repenting to God for all our sins
And keep His love within
Our hearts, minds, bodies and souls
While not ever letting the devil take control

Keep On Dreaming

Keep on dreaming and never give up
Keep on dreaming even though times get tough
Keep on dreaming even though life seems so rough
Keep on dreaming and never depart
From the Word and the love of God
Because it sets us apart
From what we call the bad and the good
Even though we are often misunderstood
For who we are as a human being
We have to keep the love of God dwelling within
Our hearts, minds, bodies and souls
And let Jesus Christ take control

Not Looking Back

Keeping the past in the past where it belongs
Because I'm going to travel to different time zones
I will set the standard of many variations of tones
Tones of being the head and not the tail
Tones of being the lender and not the borrower
Tones of being above and not beneath
Tones of having many more defeats
In not letting things repeat
Continually not looking back
And praying that God keeps the devil under my feet
By stomping and walking all over his head
While I stay strong and not afraid

You Don’t Know

You don’t know my daily struggle
You look at me and I seem to be fine
But you really don’t know what’s really on my mind
Life’s daily struggles of what to do
You really don’t have a clue
Of how I’ve survived
I push, I strive
To do my best
And praying that God will give me rest
In my mind of not worrying to death
Because yes, I am truly, truly blessed!!!

Have You Ever???

Have you ever been to a place
Where you didn't know what to do?
Of having feelings of being
So lost, lonely, and blue?
Feeling blue from your emotions and circumstances
Praying to God to give you a second chance
Of getting your life back on track
And not having any more lack
From being homeless and without?
Lord, without a doubt
I will give a great big shout
Of praise for making a way
And for the blessings not having a delay

May 18, 2016

It's the day of restoration
Restoration of all the abuse and torment
In being in an abusive marriage
Almost seventeen years
Seventeen years that's been wasted for so long
Now it's time for me to go to another zone
Of happiness, love, honor and respect
While not having any more regrets
Of "I should have" or "I could have"
Now my life is up for grabs
Grabbing and snatching back
What's been taken from me as a woman
And human being
While finally making amends
Amends to the woman that I'm becoming
Looking so very stunning!
From my head to my toes
I'm continuing to live life and follow my goals
Of making a better living for me and my family
And not continuing to do a lot of rambling
Rambling and complaining

From all my past hurts and pains
But continuing to find strength to sustain
From who I once was
And now the woman I'm becoming
A very nice, beautiful, independent individual
With a lot of hopes, dreams, and goals
I'm completely being healed from the depth of my soul

Restore Me, Lord

From the crown of my head to the soles of my feet
I shall feel no more defeat
From the innermost part of my heart
I will have a brand new start
From the whole being of me
I will be free
To live for God in peace
Watch my faith continue to increase
As I continue to run this race
Of restoration and wholeness
Still standing up with a lot of boldness
Holding my head up so high
So high to the sky
And yes, I do reply
To what was and is to come
I'm thankful to God for His only begotten Son
His name is Jesus Christ
And you should get Him in your life

A Tug of War

Battling in the spirit as well as the natural
Keeping your eyes on the Lord
And praying for Him to bring you out
Without a doubt
Just begin to shout
For victory, joy, and your breakthrough
The Lord truly knows what to do
Keep your mind stayed on him
Not the problem or situation at hand
Because Jesus Christ is the man
With all of the plans
So don't worry anymore on how He's going to bring you out
Like I said before
Just begin to shout
That the victory has been won
Because God gave His only begotten Son
To set us free from the war within us
And in Him we can find trust
Trusting Him to deliver us
From this tug of war in our minds
While we stay focused and let our light shine

In this world of darkness and sin
While continuing to pray within
And pray with our hearts
Never letting the love of Jesus depart

Battle Wounds

Struggling each and every day
Mentally and sometimes physically
Praying to God to take the pain away
Praying to God to heal me
From the crown of my head to the soles of my feet
Sometimes I feel so defeated
Defeated in keeping the faith
And trusting God to do what He said He would do
Sometimes I get a little blue
The battle between my mind and my body
Sometimes takes a toll on me
But I must stand up against the devil
So he will flee
I must believe and decree that I'm healed, healthy, and whole
While letting God stay in control
Of my every situation
Without hesitation
Because He has already given me a revelation
Of what's to come
If I believe and keep my mind stayed on Him

He promised to keep me in perfect peace
And I know that with time
All things are made whole and new again
So I keep praying within
Praying with my heart each and every day
Because I've been wounded in so many ways
I've been wounded with insecurities
In losing myself
Of loving a man that never loved me
And abused me for twenty whole years
I've been wounded with rejection and misunderstanding at times
From trying to do the right things
And always feeling like the black sheep of the family
I've been wounded with being homeless
And losing everything that I've owned
Yet praying for God to restore
I've been wounded in not having more than enough
And barely making it to survive
But I knew my God supplies all of my needs
I've been wounded from not having my father in my life
And my mother having to raise me on her own
But I've prayed to God to take away all the hurt and strife
Those are some of the obstacles I went through
And they were difficult to bare
But my battle wounds blessed me in so many ways

I'm now living in a stable place on my own
Where I can finally call home
I'm now making it with more than enough
And not barely anymore
I'm now healed from having strife
Towards my father
For not being part of my life
I'm now with a God sent, God fearing man
And husband
Who loves and adores me for me
When I thought I would never find love again
And that true love really exists
I'm now healed from all my insecurities
Because I know who I am and Who's I am
I am a child of the Most High God
I am a beautiful, smart, and bright young lady
With high self-esteem
I no longer feel like the black sheep of the family
Because ei gave it all to the Lord
I'm now healthy, whole, and healed
From the crown of my head to the soles of my feet
Because God, indeed, is a healer of all infirmities
Always remember
Your battle wounds are not intended to weaken you
But they come to make you stronger than before
That's how you grow and encourage someone else

Thanking God that the battle has been won

And "Victory is mine, says the Lord."

I would like to dedicate this poem to my husband, Joseph LaRoyce Jackson Sr. and my daughter Shakia Renece Locklear for helping me with the title and some of the words. Thank you both so much. God bless!

From The Kitchen to the Upper Room

From the kitchen to the upper room is where you're at
Putting in all those long hours
Of hard work, blood, sweat, and tears
Indeed, a fact
A fact in the matter that you didn't give up
In doing the will of God by using your hands
Yes, it brought on great demands
Demands of your time, endurance, and patience
Yes, you've started a great revelation
In God's great plans for your many talents and gifts
Sometimes you need to be uplifted
In your mind and heart
But never let anyone or anything tear you apart
From using your God given talents and rights
I could only imagine it was a fight
In being the person that you are
Now you're that bright, shining star
Now it's all yours for the taking
The taking for your heart's desire
Just remember to always try
To do your best

And remember to worry much less

Dedicated to: Evangelist Daphne Freeman

A Blessing Delayed is Not Denied

A blessing delayed is not denied
Even though sometimes you do get a little tired
In wondering when will it ever come
Praying to God to keep you calm
Calming your emotions and your thoughts
It will seem like everything is at a halt
A halt to what's to come
While setting your esteems
So far beyond your wildest dreams
And imaginations
And giving God all the glory without any hesitations
Believing and standing on God's word and faithfulness
Just keep on believing
Because it's only a test of your gratefulness
And of your faith and your endurance
To hold on like a strong soldier that you are
Striving to become that bright, shining star
That you're meant to be
And praying to God to make the devil flee
From your mind, thoughts and soul
While finally taking all of the control

In taking back your high self-esteem
And faithfulness in God
And pray to never depart
From the love of God
That He has shown to us all
Remember to keep the faith and not fall

Shine Bright Like a Diamond

Shine bright like the diamond that you are
Keep on reaching and shooting for the stars
Of hope, love, and success
Also remember that you are truly blessed
From the crown of your head to the soles of your feet
Just know, you won't feel any defeat
No defeat to how you're going to make it
And succeed in your everyday life
Remember to let go of all the hurt and strife
From the ones that did you wrong
Just let go and move on
To another zone
Of happiness and hope
Remember that you are dope
In not panicking and giving up on yourself
Now you can step back and put your mind at rest
Because this too is only a test
Of your faith in God
Because that's where it all starts

Dear Lord, Protect, Hide, Cover, and Keep

Dear Lord
Protect, hide, cover, and keep us
In Your will and in Your care
Let us know that You're always there
To keep Your angels of protection all around us
Yes Lord, in You we can trust
With our life in your hands
Yes Lord, You bring on great demands
Great demands of love that You show us each and every day
Lord, we thank You for making a way
Out of no way
Lord, we thank You for not letting us go astray
From Your love
Which is as sweet as a dove
That comes from above
In the heavens and under the earth
Yes, Lord, sometimes we do need a rebirth
Of Your Holy Spirit
So that we won't begin to feel so weary
From the cares of the world

Lord please just keep us

Every man, woman, boy, and girl

LORD, PLEASE BREAK EVERY CHAIN!!!!!

Lord, please break every chain of defeat
Letting us go while You take all the heat
Of bondage, hurt, and pain
Lord, we know in You our strength will be gained
From dealing with everyday life
Lord bless us to stop all of the anger and strife
In being let down and overlooked
By our so called family and peers
Lord please take away all of our fears
The fear of sometimes being all alone
Lord, You just have to set the tone
Of Your loving arms wrapped all around us
Because in You we can find trust
Trusting You to see us through
All of the hurt, sorrow, and pain
While keeping the faith to stay sane
In our hearts, minds, and emotions
Lord, we must continue to say our daily devotions
Of the Word of God
While pushing to never depart

From Your love that you show us each and every day
Lord, please don't let us go astray
No matter how hard things may get
Lord, just remind us that we can't quit
Quitting is not the solution
But keeping the faith and trusting God
Is our greatest resolution

Summer

The time of year
To kick back and enjoy yourself
With family and friends that's dear
To your heart
Taking road trips and never depart
From enjoying the beginnings of those trips until the end
That sounds like a big win
In coming together and having so much fun
In the sun
And in going beyond
In taking so many pictures
To remember those great memories that you've captured
Just remember that life is very natural

Spring

A beautiful time of the year
In which everything seems so clear
Even though pollen and bugs are always near
To keep you off track and distracted
Because this is the time of year that they're very proactive
To the flowers blooming all over the world
Wishing peace and blessings
To every man, woman, boy, and girl!!!

GOD'S GRACE

God's grace is on us each and every day
Lord, we thank You for always making a way
Out of no way
Lord, please help up to stay focused
And continue to pray
For Your grace and mercy towards us each day
Lord, please never let us go astray
From Your love and tender care
Lord, we dare not praise You
Because You're always there
For the good times and the bad
Lord, sometimes we get a little sad
From so much going on in this sinful world
Lord, please keep every man, woman, boy, and girl
Keep us in Your will and in Your care
Because sometimes life doesn't seem fair

In The Midnight Hour

Late in the midnight hour
God's going to turn it around
For your good
Because you've always stood
In the faith of not giving up
Sometimes, yes, you've fell in a rut
Of helplessness, loneliness, and defeat
But I bow down and decree
The blessings and the Will of God
Bowing on my knees
Praying to God to make the devil flee
From my finances and health problems too
At times, I've felt so lost, lonely, and blue
Knowing all the time that God was my clue
In keeping the faith and not giving up
Even though sometimes it gets tough
But remember
Late in the midnight hour
That's when God's work is at hand
So be blessed and always stand
On the Word of God

IN THE MIDST OF THE STORM AND LIFE STRUGGLES

And never, ever depart

Dedicated to Pastor Steven Bradley

FLASHBACK PRAISES!!!!

Look back over your life
Thanking and praising God for bringing you out
Of so many obstacles
Ups and downs that you've gone through
Oh yes, it's true
God really does love you
From the crowns of your head to the soles of your feet
God loves you because He saved you from so much defeat
From everyday life and unnecessary changes
Thank God for sending you His guardian angels
From the heavens
To the earth
Thank God for removing the curse
Of lying, stealing
Adultery and fornication too
Yes, it's true
That you didn't have a clue
How you would come out of your situations and mess
Yes, I thank God it was only a test
Of your faith, dreams, and hopes
Jesus saved you in time

Before you eloped from His mercy
And saving grace
Now He's giving you strength
To continue to run this race

Dedicated to: Mother Flowers
Emmanuel Temple Church of God in Christ

Diary of a Mad, Black, and Angry Woman, Part Two

Part two is what they used to call me
Yes, it's true
I've lived this life and didn't even really have a clue
To how I was going to make it out in one piece
I prayed to God to keep my mind at ease
Easing my heart and mind from so much hurt and pain
And praying to not let things remain
A bitter, black, angry woman
I felt myself sinking and going under
Under life stress from a man
That put me through so much hurt and heartaches
I keep praying to the Lord for my sake
The sake of staying sane in my mind
I said to myself, "I must get it together and unwind"
Because I couldn't continue to go through this
And leave my children behind
Falling into the hands of an angry man
God stepped in on time
Because He had a great plan
For my life at hand

I had to finally let go and take that stand
In taking back my life
To let go of all the anger and strife
That has built up for so many years
Yes, I cried and shed so many tears
From all of the abuse
I felt so neglected and misused
From a man that I thought loved me
I had to just let go and let it be
Praying to God to just set me free
From all the hurt and disappointments
God stepped in on time
To let me know it's only for a moment
A moment in time
My life is back to being mine

Part Two

LIMITLESS THANKS

I'm thankful for all the things
That God has brought me through
I didn't have a clue
Of what was to come
I prayed to stay so calm
Calming my spirit down with the peace of God
Praying for it to never depart
Thankful for a second chance at life
Not holding on to anymore strife
From the things that I've been through
And not continuing to feel so lost, lonely, and blue
I'm thankful to God
For delivering me from the hands of a man
That physically, mentally, and emotionally
Abused me for over twenty years
Twenty years of brokenness and defeat
I thank God for stepping in
And not letting things repeat
I thank God for bringing me out of so many things
And for building up my self-esteem
An esteem that was once taken

Now I'm that start in the making

Of a new beginning

Oh yes indeed, I'm winning!!!

I'm winning back everything that was taken from me

Yes, it will be

Because Jesus Christ has set me free!!!!

PUT A PRAISE ON IT!!!!!

When life seems so hard to bear
And sometimes it seems like no one cares
Put a praise on it!!!!
When bills are due
And you don't even have a clue
To how things will get done
Put a praise on it!!!!
When life seems to get the best of you
With your finances, health, and family too
Put a praise on it!!!!
Life can sometimes bring you down
But remember that Jesus is around
Put a praise on it!!!!
Stand still and God will see you through
And remember that a praying family is the clue
You will be forever bonded like glue
I pray that nothing ever tears you apart
And that it's the beginning of a brand new start
Put a praise on it!!!!

He's Crying Out

He's crying out from all the hurt, sorrow, and pain
Praying and seeking God's face for the strength he will gain
Gaining more wisdom and knowledge
Of how to let things go
He's praying to God and staying with the flow
Of everyday life
As he's leaning on his beautiful wife
To help him through this process of being free
He prays often and stays on his knees
Bowing down to the heavens above
One day you'll receive peace just like the dove
Peace from trying to do it on your own
Just remember, you've got to let go
And let God take you to that zone
Of peace, happiness, and salvation in your heart
Keep praying and seeking God's face and never depart

Dedicated to my husband: Joseph LaRoyce Jackson, Sr.

Going Through The Storms

Going through the storms of life
Whether it's naturally or spiritually
They can sometimes bring you down
Just remember to take off that sad little frown
Of life's struggles
For one day it'll be just a tuggle
Of life's lessons
They can bring about great blessings
As you endure through the pain and confusion
This, too, is an illusion
Of all the suffering you have to go through
So just stay true
To God and yourself
And please don't worry to death
About how things are going to happen and when
Because worrying is a sin
Of self-destruction and fear
Just remember to always keep God near and dear
To your heart
And never, ever depart
From God's love

All things come from up above

In the skies

And beyond the earth

Because sometimes we need a rebirth

In all men

And remember, we can't continue to sin

VOLUMES OF THE HEART

Volumes of the heart are a part of everyday life
Letting go and not thinking twice
About everything that's going on
Just keep stepping into another zone
Of peace and reflection
Praying for more direction
Of how to be a better you
Even though sometimes you won't even have a clue
On where to start
Sometimes things fall apart
From not listening to the volumes of your heart
So never depart
From the love of God
Keep Him first and foremost through it all
Through all your hurts and disappointments
Remember, this too is only for a moment
A moment in time
So let go and unwind
And listen to those musical chimes
Of your heart
Keep on pushing to a brand new start

Made in the USA
Columbia, SC
26 May 2019